How to use this book

Follow the advice, in italics, given for you on each page.
Support the children as they read the text that is shaded in cream.
***Praise** the children at every step!*
Detailed guidance is provided in the Read Write Inc. Phonics Handbook.

9 reading activities

Children:

1. *Practise reading the speed sounds.*
2. *Read the green, red and challenge words for the non-fiction text.*
3. *Listen as you read the introduction.*
4. *Discuss the vocabulary check with you.*
5. *Read the non-fiction text.*
6. *Re-read the non-fiction text and discuss the 'questions to talk about'.*
7. *Re-read the non-fiction text with fluency and expression.*
8. *Answer the questions to 'read and answer'.*
9. *Practise reading the speed words.*

Speed sounds

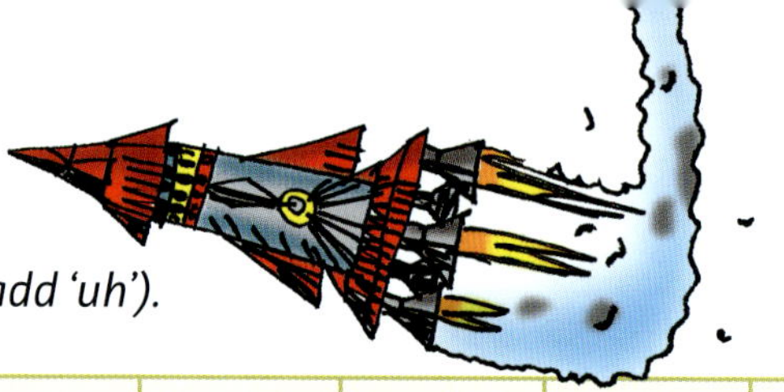

Consonants *Say the pure sounds (do not add 'uh').*

f ff	l **ll**	m **mm**	n nn kn	r **rr** wr	s ss **se**	v ve	z zz **se**	sh	th	ng nk

b bb	c k **ck**	d **dd**	g gg	h	j g ge	p pp	qu	t tt	w wh	x	y	ch tch

Vowels *Say the vowel sound and then the word, eg 'a', 'at'.*

at	hen head	in	on	up	day	see happy	high find	blow no

zoo	look	car	for door snore	fair	whirl	shout	boy spoil

*Each box contains one sound but sometimes more than one grapheme. Focus graphemes are **circled**.*

Green words

Read in Fred Talk (pure sounds).

sort	fork	jar	large	scoop	spoon	chop	cheese	
green	next	bright	salad	cress	first	bowl	them	add
stir	pick	way						

Read in syllables.

sweet\` corn	→	sweetcorn	a\` dult	→	adult
yell\` ow	→	yellow	past\` a	→	pasta
carr\` ot	→	carrot	yumm\` y	→	yummy

Read the root word first and then with the ending.

cut	→	cutting	dress	→	dressing	cook	→	cooked
shell	→	shelled	bow	→	bows	chunk	→	chunks

Red words

the to great you of some

any now into want your

A sweetcorn salad

Introduction

Do you like sweetcorn? Do you like salads? Have you ever prepared something to eat? In this book you'll see how to make a sweetcorn salad – healthy and yummy!

Written by Gill Munton

Vocabulary check

Discuss the meaning (as used in the non-fiction text) after the children have read the word.

	definition
shelled	*with the shell taken off*
radishes	*hot-tasting vegetable that you eat raw*
dressing	*a kind of sauce that you put on salad*
scoop	*take out with a spoon*

Punctuation to note:

First Chop	*Capital letters that start sentences*
.	*Full stop at the end of each sentence*
!	*Exclamation marks to show that something is very important*
:	*Colon to show that a list is next*
•	*Bullet point to show each thing in a list*

This is the way to mix up a great salad.

Ask an adult to help you with the cutting.

Salad is good for you!

You will need:

- a can of bright yellow sweetcorn
- 2 eggs (cooked and shelled)
- pasta bows (cooked)
- some chunks of cheese

- a carrot
- radishes or nuts (any sort)
- fresh green cress
- a jar of garlic salad dressing.

1 First, scoop the sweetcorn into a large bowl.

2 Chop up the eggs and tip them in.

3 Next, add the pasta bows and the cheese.

4 Cut up the carrot and put it in the bowl.

5 Now add the radishes or nuts and stir them in with a large spoon.

6 Add the cress.

7 Tip some salad dressing into the bowl and mix up the salad.

8 If you want, add more cress on top.

9 Now pick up your fork! Yummy!

Questions to talk about

Re-read the page. Read the question to the children. Tell them whether it is a FIND IT *question or* PROVE IT *question.*

FIND IT	PROVE IT
✓ *Turn to the page*	✓ *Turn to the page*
✓ *Read the question*	✓ *Read the question*
✓ *Find the answer*	✓ *Find your evidence*
	✓ *Explain why*

Page 9:	FIND IT	*What should an adult help you to do?*
Page 11:	FIND IT	*What can you use instead of radishes?*
Pages 12–13:	FIND IT	*What do you add after the eggs?*
Page 13:	FIND IT	*What do you do with the carrot before you put it in the bowl?*
Page 15:	FIND IT	*What is the last thing you put on top of the salad?*
Page 16:	PROVE IT	*Why do you need a fork?*
Page 16:	PROVE IT	*Do you think you would enjoy the salad? (Why? Why not?)*

Questions to read and answer

(Children complete without your help.)

1 Salad is **good** / **bad** / **cooked** for you.

2 You will need pasta **bowls** / **bows** / **chunks**.

3 You will need some **shelled** / **fresh** / **bright** green cress.

4 The eggs must be cooked and **shelled** / **filled** / **scooped**.

5 Stir in the radishes with a **spoon** / **carrot** / **bowl**.